# WOLVERINES

Printed in the United States of America,
North Mankato, Minnesota
052012
092012

 THIS BOOK CONTAINS AT LEAST 10% RECYCLED MATERIALS.

Editor: Chrös McDougall
Series Designer: Craig Hinton

**Photo Credits:** Duane Burleson/AP Images, cover; AP Images, 1, 12, 18, 21, 23, 25, 31, 33, 42 (top), 42 (bottom left), 42 (bottom right); Michael Young/AP Images, 4, 10; Tony Ding/AP Images, 6, 41, 43 (bottom right); Carlos Osorio/AP Images, 9, 29; Bettmann/Corbis/AP Images, 17, 43 (top); Mark Duncan/AP Images, 26; Tom DiPace/AP Images, 34, 43 (bottom left); Albert Dickson/Sporting News/AP Images, 37; Mark J. Terrill/AP Images, 39; Bill Fundaro/AP Images, 44

**Library of Congress Cataloging-in-Publication Data**
Rappoport, Ken.
Michigan Wolverines / by Ken Rappoport.
p. cm. -- (Inside college football)
ISBN 978-1-61783-498-1
1. Michigan Wolverines (Football team)--History--Juvenile literature. 2. University of Michigan--Football--History--Juvenile literature. I. Title.
GV958.U52863R36 2013
796.332'630977435--dc23

2012001851

# TABLE OF CONTENTS


1 BIG GAME IN THE BIG HOUSE ........ 5

2 A MICHIGAN MAN ........ 13

3 RUN FOR THE ROSES ........ 19

4 THE GREATEST RIVALRY ........ 27

5 BACK ON TOP ........ 35

TIMELINE 42

QUICK STATS 44

QUOTES & ANECDOTES 45

GLOSSARY 46

FOR MORE INFORMATION 47

INDEX 48

ABOUT THE AUTHOR 48

**The lights were turned on for Michigan Stadium's first night game when the Wolverines played Notre Dame in 2011.**

# BIG GAME IN THE BIG HOUSE

**EXCITEMENT FILLED THE AIR. ON SEPTEMBER 10, 2011, FANS WERE ABOUT TO SEE SOMETHING THEY HAD NEVER BEFORE WITNESSED IN MICHIGAN STADIUM. FOR THE FIRST TIME IN THE UNIVERSITY OF MICHIGAN WOLVERINES' 131-YEAR FOOTBALL HISTORY, THE LIGHTS WERE ON IN THE "BIG HOUSE," THE NICKNAME FOR THE STADIUM. AND NOT ONLY WAS IT THE FIRST NIGHT GAME IN ANN ARBOR, MICHIGAN, BUT IT WAS ALSO A MEETING WITH A FIERCE RIVAL—THE NOTRE DAME FIGHTING IRISH.**

The result was an unbelievable, heart-stopping experience. A record crowd of 114,804 filled the famous stadium. That is as large as the population of many US cities. It did not matter that both programs had not matched up to past glories. A Michigan-Notre Dame battle was always a hot ticket.

Michigan's program was a storied success. The Wolverines had won 11 national championships and

**Michigan sophomore wide receiver Jeremy Gallon runs downfield against Notre Dame in 2011.**

42 conference titles to that point. A losing season in the Big Ten Conference was rare for Michigan. After all, Michigan had more victories than anyone in college football. However, the Wolverines had losing seasons in 2008 and 2009 and were just 7–6 in 2010.

Like Michigan, Notre Dame was hoping to rebound after several subpar years. The Michigan-Notre Dame rivalry started in 1887. It had long been an important part of college football. Going into the 2011 game, Michigan led the series 22–15–1.

This game was also special because of the historic importance of the Big House lights. Ticket prices had jumped higher and higher, ranging from $185 to $600.

The famous stadium was built in 1927. Since then, all-time greats such as Tommy Harmon, Bennie Oosterbaan, and US President Gerald Ford had starred wearing the Wolverines' colors—maize and blue.

As the players raced onto the Big House turf for the 2011 game, they were greeted by a "maize out," which is a sea of yellow shirts in the stands. The sound of "The Victors," Michigan's fight song, filled the stadium along with the cheers of pom-pom-waving fans.

But the joyful mood soon turned to despair. Michigan fell behind, and the Fighting Irish controlled the game. Notre Dame outgained Michigan 268–90 yards to take a 17–7 lead. The Irish had 15 first downs to the Wolverines' three. Then the Irish pushed their lead to 24-7 with 2:13 left in the third quarter.

But Michigan would not give up. The Wolverines scored one touchdown, and then another. The team then scored a third when junior quarterback Denard Robinson fired a 21-yard touchdown pass to junior

**DID YOU KNOW?**

Through 2011, the Michigan Wolverines' 894 wins were the most of any college football program in the United States. The Wolverines' record of 894–310–36 (.735) also was the all-time highest winning percentage.

## HISTORIC HELMET

When Fritz Crisler brought the unique "winged" helmet to Michigan in 1938, he wanted it to bring attention. And it did just that. The helmet was not only different but also had a practical advantage on the field, according to Crisler. He was convinced the bright yellow (maize) wing on a blue background would help Michigan's passers better see receivers downfield.

"There was a tendency to use different colored helmets just for receivers in those days," Crisler said, "but I always thought that would be as helpful for the defense as for the offense." Michigan made a successful debut wearing the new helmet when it opened the 1938 season with a 14–0 win over Michigan State.

There have been a few minor changes to the design over the years. And other Michigan sports teams such as ice hockey, baseball, softball, field hockey, and even rowing later adopted the winged helmet.

wide receiver Vincent Smith. They took their first lead of the night, 28–24, with 1:12 to go in the fourth quarter.

But the game was not over. Notre Dame retook the lead, 31–28, on a 29-yard touchdown pass from Tommy Rees to Theo Riddick.

Only 30 seconds remained. It seemed only a miracle could save the day for the Wolverines. Or a defensive blunder by the Irish. And that is just what happened.

Michigan sophomore wide receiver Jeremy Gallon was left unguarded by the Irish defenders. Robinson saw him wide open. Taking advantage, he fired a pass to his receiver. Gallon completed a 64-yard play before he was tackled.

Watching from the sidelines, one Michigan player said, "Whoa, how did this happen?" Notre Dame had to be feeling the same way.

Now the ball was on the Notre Dame 16-yard line, with eight seconds

Michigan wide receiver Roy Roundtree catches the game-winning touchdown against Notre Dame in 2011.

left in the game. Michigan coach Brady Hoke had a choice. He could kick a field goal and send the game into overtime, or he could go for a touchdown to win the game. What would the Wolverines do?

"Coach took a stab," junior wide receiver Roy Roundtree said.

Hoke called a pass play. Roundtree ran a pattern to the right side of the end zone. The team's leading receiver in 2010, Roundtree was still looking for his first pass reception of the night. He battled for position in the end zone against a Notre Dame cornerback.

"I just jumped in air and focused on it, made sure my foot was down," Roundtree said.

**Michigan quarterback Denard Robinson celebrates with fans after the 2011 win over Notre Dame.**

Soaring up under the lights, Roundtree caught the ball and landed with his foot inside the white line.

"It was like, 'Man, I just caught the winning touchdown,'" he said.

The final score left Michigan on top 35–31. Robinson starred with 338 yards and four passing touchdowns, along with 108 rushing yards and a rushing touchdown.

"It was kind of crazy," Robinson said. "I've never scored like that."

The crowd erupted in Michigan's fight song, clapping and running onto the field to embrace players. Players jumped into the stands, hugging the fans. It was undoubtedly an exciting finish. And in 131 years of football, the Wolverines had produced a number of exciting finishes. It all began in 1879. Michigan football then came of age in 1901, featuring unusual passes and a pioneering coach concerned with time.

It was time for "Hurry Up" Yost.

**MICHIGAN FIRSTS**

The Michigan football team played its first home game in 1883. That year, the Wolverines beat the Detroit Independents 40–5. In their first home game in Michigan Stadium, the Wolverines played Ohio Wesleyan. Michigan won the game 33–0 in front of 17,483 fans on October 1, 1927.

Michigan coach Fielding Yost was renowned for quickly turning around football programs.

# A MICHIGAN MAN

**"HURRY UP, HURRY UP!" IT WAS 1901—22 YEARS AFTER THE SCHOOL'S FIRST INTERCOLLEGIATE FOOTBALL GAME—AND MICHIGAN'S NEW FOOTBALL COACH, FIELDING YOST, WAS DRIVING HIS TEAM HARD.**

Football then hardly resembled the game played today. It looked much more like rugby. And Yost's style was much different from the way Michigan usually played football: slow offenses with massive line assaults. Yost believed that a team with speed and agility could exhaust opponents. So he had the Wolverines play fast with groundbreaking offensive game plans. Yost's strategy featured the forward pass, which was foreign to most football teams at the time.

Yost had quite an unusual background when he applied for the coaching job at Michigan. In 1900, he coached four different teams on the West Coast *in the same year*, including Stanford. Michigan officials were impressed with Yost's ability to quickly turn around a football program. So they hired him to coach the Wolverines. No one expected what happened next.

The Wolverines opened the 1901 season with a 55–0 victory over Albion and a 57–0 win over Case. Later in the season, the Wolverines posted a 128–0 victory over Buffalo. The Wolverines rang up 22 touchdowns in just 50 minutes of football in a game that had to be stopped early. The Buffalo players had aches all over their bodies. Many were injured. They were relieved to go home early after the brutal pounding they took from the powerful Wolverines.

Michigan was not only rolling up points at a rapid pace, but it was also not allowing its opponents to score. The Wolverines finished the 1901 season without giving up a single point. Teams around the country were amazed. News of Michigan's awesome record started filtering in. The team had a 10–0 record and had outscored opponents 501–0.

**FOOTBALL BEGINNINGS**

It was a hot Memorial Day in 1879 and the crowd was ready to see something new. Football had come to Chicago. An enthusiastic crowd headed out to White Stocking Park to watch the new game. Michigan was playing its first game of intercollegiate football. The Wolverines' opponent was Racine, a small college in Wisconsin.

From the start, Michigan players seemed to have a better grasp of the game than their opponents. A Racine newspaper noted the problems the hometown players were having.

"Our boys showed sadly deficient in playing together, that is they did not understand how to pass the ball from one to another," it reported.

The game was a loose combination of rugby and football. Irving Kane Pond scored the first touchdown for Michigan. The crowd responded with cheers of "Pond forever." Michigan went on to a 1–0 victory. Football was on its way at Michigan.

Players in those days played both defense and offense. That season, Neil Snow was a fullback and defensive end for Michigan. He was captain of the team and an All-American. Snow had played one of his greatest games in the 1898 victory over Chicago that inspired Michigan's fight song, "The Victors." Another player, Harrison "Boss" Weeks, was an obvious leader. Yost moved him into the quarterback position. Halfback Willie Heston was another star. Heston's reflexes and strength were legendary. He finished with 71 career touchdowns.

Michigan's 1901 season was impressive. In four of the Wolverines' 10 games, the opposing team never had the ball in Michigan territory. Northwestern was the only team that got as far as Michigan's 35-yard line. The Wolverines' playmaking speed crippled opponents.

Michigan's next stop was the Rose Bowl. The Rose Bowl remains one of the most famous bowl games, and the Big Ten conference champion still plays there most years. Michigan played Stanford, the Pacific Coast champion, in the first-ever Rose Bowl that year. In the pre-game parade, the Michigan players rode in a large carriage wearing maize and blue uniforms and waving colorful Wolverine banners. At Tournament Park, 8,500 spectators turned out to see the battle of football giants.

Playing under a blazing sun with temperatures in the mid-80s, Stanford made two goal-line stands. The California team turned Michigan away until late in the first half. Finally, Heston broke away for a 21-yard run to put the ball on Stanford's 8-yard line. Then Snow burst over the goal line for the first touchdown in Rose Bowl history. It started a landslide of points for Michigan. Snow added four more touchdowns in the second half. And Heston gained 170 yards rushing as the Wolverines buried Stanford 49–0.

With eight minutes still to play, Stanford captain Ralph Fisher walked over to the Michigan bench. He consulted with Wolverines captain Hugh White. "If you are willing, sir, we'll call it a day," Fisher said.

It had been a brutal contest. One Stanford lineman, a cousin of President Theodore Roosevelt, had suffered a broken leg. And he kept playing until he fractured three ribs. Stanford had no reserves left.

The Wolverines finished with an 11–0 record. They outscored their opponents 550–0. And they were recognized as national co-champions along with Harvard. Various polls, such as the Associated Press (AP) Poll, determined the national champion at the time.

In 1902, the Wolverines outscored their opponents 644–12 and won all 11 games for another national championship. Michigan again had unbeaten seasons and national titles in 1903, 1904, 1918, and 1923. The Wolverines became known as college football's "Point a Minute" team, and their coach was known as "Hurry Up" Yost.

### FIELDING YOST

During his 25 years as coach of Michigan football, Fielding Yost led the Wolverines to six national championships. It would be hard to top his first five years at the Wolverines' helm, in which he lost only one of 57 games. Later, as Michigan's athletic director, Yost was the driving force behind many new sports facilities on campus, including his pride and joy—monster-sized Michigan Stadium.

**Benny Friedman was one of the key players on Fielding Yost's "best team ever" in 1925.**

Despite the numerous championships, it was a team that did not win the national championship that Yost considered his "best team ever." That was the 1925 squad featuring the great passing combination of Benny Friedman and Bennie Oosterbaan. Only a 3–2 loss to Northwestern in an unusually low-scoring game prevented Michigan from finishing with a perfect record.

Yost's retirement after the 1926 season was the end of an era at Michigan. Under coach Harry Kipke, Michigan won back-to-back national titles in 1932 and 1933. And soon, a new player arrived to begin another dominant era in Ann Arbor.

an standout halfback Tom Harmon
ainst Pennsylvania during a 1940

3

# RUN FOR THE ROSES

**THERE WAS NO STOPPING TOM HARMON. IT WAS THE 1940 SEASON, AND THE MICHIGAN SUPERSTAR HALFBACK WAS RUNNING WILD.**

"Very seldom did one man tackle Tom," said teammate Forest "Evy" Evashevski. "It took one man to slow him down, and then the others could pile on."

If they could catch him, that is. Harmon was known for awesome plays that left tacklers in the dust. One afternoon while facing Penn, he was trapped at the line of scrimmage. Harmon retreated 25 yards toward his own goal line. From one sideline to the other, he cut and twisted. Tacklers lunged at him. But he escaped. Finally, he broke free and headed out to the open field. Touchdown! Harmon had covered some 150 yards for that score.

In 1940, the summer before his senior year, Harmon worked as a lifeguard. He had fun running up and down the

### "AT ANY TIME"

The words "at any time" allowed modern-day football to develop. It was wartime in the 1940s. Many players went off to war. Michigan's football team was having difficulty filling its roster. Football at this time was an "iron man" game. The players remained on the field for the full 60 minutes. They played both offense and defense with no breaks. If a player left the game he could not return in the same quarter. So before a game ended it was easy to run out of players.

Michigan coach Fritz Crisler asked for help. The National Collegiate Athletic Association (NCAA) approved a rule. It permitted a substitute to enter the game "at any time." The free substitution rule allowed players to move freely in and out of the game. It was the beginning of two-platoon football, in which different players play offense and defense. Crisler became known as the "father of the two-platoon system."

sand for at least an hour a day, but he worked hard. He was in great shape for the start of the season. The Wolverines opened against the California Bears on the West Coast. Today teams travel by plane all the time. But it was rare in 1940. Instead of taking the train like usual, the Michigan football team flew to the West Coast. The Wolverines became the first intercollegiate football team to do so. It was exciting. Any team member under 21 had to get his parents' permission.

At the game, a surprise was being planned for Harmon. Evashevski waved away Harmon while he huddled with the rest of the team. Secretly, he told the team that it was Harmon's birthday. "Let's give him a present by everybody knocking somebody down." Harmon then took the opening kickoff 94 yards for a touchdown. His team had come through for him. The Wolverines went on to a 41–0 victory. "It was a firecracker start to a great year," Harmon said.

Harmon's all-around performance against Ohio State in the last game of his college career helped him clinch the Heisman Trophy. Harmon did everything. He scored three touchdowns and passed for two more. He kicked four extra points, intercepted three passes, and punted for an average of 50 yards. A thunderous ovation from the opposing fans greeted Harmon as he left the field victorious. Michigan won 40–0.

During the early 1940s, World War II brought changes to Michigan. The Ann Arbor campus was the site of a military officer training program. In the fall of 1943, more than 4,000 men in uniform were on

the Michigan campus. Among them were dozens of football players. Now playing for coach Fritz Crisler at Michigan was Elroy "Crazy Legs" Hirsch. He had been one of the country's top players at Wisconsin.

Hirsch made a bet he would score against his former teammates. As fate would have it, he was sitting on the sideline with a shoulder injury when Michigan played Wisconsin. But it was no matter. He had a solution. Into the game he went, and he kicked the final point. He won his bet, and Michigan won the game.

During the war years, players came and went. They had to leave school to go off to war. So finding experienced players became a problem for Michigan and Crisler. But then they all came back. In 1945, the war was over. Crisler had his pick of candidates. By that time, players were playing on one side of the ball, either offense or defense, not both.

Bob Chappuis was one of the players who returned to Michigan. The triple-threat back had played on a 7–3 Michigan team in 1942 before

### MAD MAGICIANS

The 1947 Michigan team was known as the "Mad Magicians." Under Fritz Crisler, the Wolverines baffled opponents with a number of offensive formations. "Sometimes, watching from the side lines, even Coach Crisler isn't sure which Michigan man has the ball," reported *Time* magazine. Sometimes, as many as five players would handle the ball on one play. The sleight-of-hand artists in the backfield included Bob Chappuis, Bump Elliott, Howard Yerges, and Jack Weisenburger. Together they worked magic, leading Michigan to an undefeated season and the national championship.

going off to war. Michigan now also had other talented players four and five deep at just about every position.

But none of them stood out like Chappuis. He was honored as the Wolverines' Most Valuable Player in 1946. The 1947 team featured the "dream" backfield of Chappuis, Charles "Bump" Elliott, Howard Yerges, and Jack Weisenburger.

By the time the regular season ended with a 21–0 victory over Ohio State, the Wolverines had carved out a 9–0 record. They were headed to the Rose Bowl. Their opponent was the University of Southern California (USC) Trojans. With Chappuis leading the way, the Wolverines produced a record 491 yards on offense. And they won 49–0. The score was identical to their first Rose Bowl after the 1901 season.

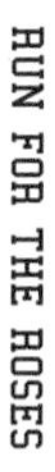

The Rose Bowl victory confirmed the top ranking for Michigan. Some were calling it the greatest Michigan team of all time. Another national championship followed. The 1948 team, under coach Bennie Oosterbaan, was voted number one after a 9–0 season. All-American quarterback Pete Elliott led the Wolverines that season.

The 1950 season ended in a Rose Bowl appearance for the Wolverines. It was Oosterbaan's only visit to a bowl game during his 11 seasons at Michigan. In 1959, the Wolverines hired another former Michigan star to coach the team, Bump Elliott. At 34, he was the youngest coach in the Big Ten. He had a tough job. The Wolverines had only won two games in 1958. Elliott's first year as the Michigan coach was also a losing season.

Elliott felt it would take three to five years to rebuild and win a championship. He was wrong—it took six. In 1964, the Wolverines won nine games and finished first in the Big Ten. Then they routed Oregon State 34–7 in the Rose Bowl.

### TOUGH SLEDDING

Amid blizzard conditions and winds swirling up to 28 miles per hour (45 km/h), Michigan beat Ohio State in their 1950 meeting known as the "Snow Bowl." Noted Michigan halfback Chuck Ortmann said: "You'd be running, and you'd have a little traction; all of a sudden you'd hit a frozen area. Your feet would go out from under you, and you'd fall down." Wolverines halfback Leo Koceski said: "It was cold, it was nasty and it wasn't any fun." At least it was a victory, 9–3 in favor of Michigan.

**Bennie Oosterbaan was an All-American end and wide receiver at Michigan before becoming the team's coach.**

Elliott stepped down as coach following the 1968 season. It did not take Michigan long to find his replacement. And the new guy proved to be more than capable of continuing the Michigan tradition.

an players carry coach Bo
bechler off the field after a 1986
er Ohio State.

# THE GREATEST RIVALRY

**THE STORY OF BO SCHEMBECHLER AND WOODY HAYES BEGAN IN OHIO, WHICH IS KNOWN AS THE BUCKEYE STATE. SCHEMBECHLER PLAYED FOR HAYES AT MIAMI OF OHIO, AND THEN HE WAS HIS ASSISTANT AT OHIO STATE. "WOODY TAUGHT ME MORE ABOUT THE GAME THAN ANYONE COULD," SCHEMBECHLER SAID. BUT SCHEMBECHLER HAD TO MAKE A DECISION. MICHIGAN, A HATED RIVAL OF OHIO STATE, HAD OFFERED HIM THE POSITION OF HEAD COACH IN 1969.**

Hayes felt betrayed when Schembechler joined Michigan. After all, like Hayes, Schembechler had been born and raised a Buckeye. How could he go to the enemy? Hayes had once called Schembechler a friend. But that was no longer the case.

"It was a very personal rivalry," said Earle Bruce, who played for Hayes and then succeeded him as coach at Ohio State. "And for the first and only time, it was as much about the coaches as it was about the game."

### LITTLE BROWN JUG

Michigan and Minnesota play for the Little Brown Jug. It is one of the most famous football trophies in the United States. As the story goes, Michigan coach Fielding Yost carried the gray plastic jug around with him so that his players could drink fresh Ann Arbor spring water. On a 1903 visit to Minnesota, the Wolverines played to a 6–6 standstill with the Golden Gophers.

The embarrassed Michigan players, known for their high scoring, were in such a hurry to get out of town that they left the jug in Minnesota. A janitor found the jug while cleaning up the next morning. When Michigan inquired about the jug, Minnesota replied: "If you want it, come up and win it."

They have been fighting for it ever since. Today, the jug is painted half blue for Michigan and half maroon for Minnesota. All the scores are printed on it.

There was a story about Hayes on a recruiting trip to Michigan. On the way home, his car ran out of gas near the Ohio border. Hayes and another coach got out and pushed the car over the border. Then they got gas. There was no way the state of Michigan was getting "a cent of my money," Hayes said.

For 10 years, the rivalry between Hayes and Schembechler continued. It became known as the "10-Year War." During that time, from 1969 to 1978, the two coaching giants usually received more media attention than their teams every time they met.

The Michigan game was always the big one for Hayes, although he refused to say the name of the school. Hayes always referred to Michigan as "that school up north."

The record between the two schools was nearly even. Schembechler and Michigan held a 5–4–1 edge over Hayes and Ohio State. During their time, Michigan and Ohio State generally

**Michigan and Minnesota play each year for the rights to claim the famous Little Brown Jug.**

dominated the Big Ten. Schembechler and Hayes split 10 conference titles between them and finished second eight times. The Big Ten then was often referred to as "the Big 2 and Little 8." It was Michigan and Ohio State, and then everyone else.

Dozens of well-known games had been featured in the rivalry. In 1968, one year before Schembechler took over, the Buckeyes had crushed the Wolverines 50–14 on the way to the national championship. Hayes took great delight in running up the score against Michigan. Near the end of that game, he ordered his team to go for two points after a touchdown. The Wolverines and their fans were really angry. When asked why he went for two points late in a game that was already decided, Hayes quipped: "Because I couldn't go for three."

One year later, the Buckeyes were going for their second straight national championship. One game remained on their schedule—Michigan. Schembechler, in his first year, had a plan. In practices leading up to the game, he had his players wear a tiny No. 50 on their jerseys. This was a reminder of the previous year's score, 50–14. *Be angry*, he told his players. *Do not let it happen again.*

With a 22-game winning streak, the unbeaten Buckeyes were heavy favorites. Football experts were calling Ohio State unbeatable. But Schembechler was not concerned. He knew how he could beat his former boss. He had learned how from Hayes himself. Hayes had said to always attack an opponent at its strongest point. In this case, Michigan would attack Rex Kern, the Buckeyes' quarterback.

## THE BIG HOUSE

Michigan Stadium is known as the "Big House." Going into the 2012 season, the stadium's official capacity was 109,901. That is quite a difference from Regents Field, where the Wolverines once played their games at Ann Arbor. That originally seated 400. Growing interest in football forced the building of Ferry Field, which was opened in 1906. Its capacity eventually increased to 45,000. Fielding Yost made the push for a bigger stadium. Michigan Stadium was completed in 1927 at a cost of $950,000. The original seating capacity was 84,401.

"We didn't want Kern running the football," Schembechler said, "so we set our defenses to stop him."

The Buckeyes took an early 6–0 lead. Michigan came back to go ahead 7–6. Senior fullback Garvie Craw scored the first of his two touchdowns on a three-yard plunge. It was a first. During the season, Ohio State had never given up points in the first quarter.

Kern then led the Buckeyes on a 73-yard touchdown drive. But Michigan again came back on Craw's one-yard touchdown run to go ahead 14–12.

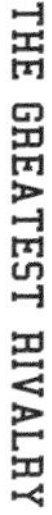

Michigan quarterback Don Moorhead, meanwhile, was having a better day than Kern. He carried the ball for 68 yards, including a one-yard touchdown run to put the Wolverines up 21–12. Tim Killian added to the Michigan lead with a 25-yard field goal later in the second quarter.

It was becoming a tough day for Kern. Michigan's secondary picked off four of his passes. By the fourth quarter, Kern was so upset that he was forced to take a seat on the bench.

"The strategy was to contain Kern," Schembechler said. With 13 minutes left, the Buckeyes were on their own 42. They needed only one yard for a first down. Kern kept the ball and ran to his left, but he was tackled for a two-yard loss. The Wolverines took over the ball and went on to a 24–12 victory. Michigan had its revenge.

Hayes was really upset. Not only did he hate losing to Michigan and his former assistant, but he lost a chance to compete for a second straight national championship. The Wolverines went on to the Rose Bowl instead. It was Schembechler's first of ten appearances in the post-season bowl known as the "granddaddy of them all."

### DOMINANT RIVALS

Ohio State and Michigan have combined to win 76 Big Ten titles and 19 national championships through 2011. In addition, they have produced 10 Heisman Trophy winners and have had more than 60 players and coaches selected into the College Football Hall of Fame.

**Bo Schembechler, *left*, and Woody Hayes had one of the most legendary rivalries in college football history.**

Coaching for 21 years at Michigan, from 1969 to 1989, Schembechler took his teams to 17 bowl games. He won 13 Big Ten titles and posted a 194–48–5 record.

Several years after Hayes retired, he was asked how he remembered Schembechler—friend or foe? "We've fought and quarreled for years, but we're great friends," Hayes said in an interview with *The Lantern* on February 10, 1986. Few rivalries ever matched that of Hayes and Schembechler.

an wide receiver Desmond
d leaps for a catch against Florida
n 1991.

5

# BACK ON TOP

**THE WOLVERINES WERE STRUGGLING. BO SCHEMBECHLER HAD RETIRED AFTER THE 1989 SEASON. GARY MOELLER TOOK OVER AND LED MICHIGAN TO THE ROSE BOWL IN HIS SECOND AND THIRD SEASONS. THEN THE WOLVERINES EMBARKED ON FOUR CONSECUTIVE SEASONS WITH FOUR LOSSES EACH. IT WAS THE WORST FOUR-YEAR STRETCH FOR MICHIGAN SINCE THE 1930s.**

"I heard the jokes about the M in Michigan standing for mediocrity," said defensive back Marcus Ray.

In 1996, Michigan finished seventh in the Big Ten in scoring and sixth in total offense. The outlook did not look any better going into the 1997 season. *Sports Illustrated* ranked the Wolverines number 18 in the country. They were just about ignored as a serious contender for the national championship.

Coach Lloyd Carr had taken over in 1995. He was looking for more offense. His star tailback, Tim Biakabutuka, had departed for the National Football League after that first season. One day before the 1997 season, Carr was leaving a dinner for recruits with Charles Woodson, his talented cornerback, when he had an idea.

"Charles," he asked, "how would you like to play some tailback?" Woodson thought about the abuse the position takes. "How about wide receiver?" Woodson countered.

It was the first day of practice. But after adding this new position to his duties, Woodson put on an all-star show. Carr was delighted. He had found the offense he was looking for. "I mean, it was the first day, and we all just went, 'Wow!'" Carr said.

At first Woodson was not sure about playing on both the offense and defense. But then he really liked it. He found he could make more plays. There were more opportunities to make an impact. "The one thing I've never liked is sitting on the sideline," he said.

### HEISMAN POSE

Ohio State should have known better than to kick the ball to Desmond Howard, Michigan's great punt return man. But in the second quarter of their game in 1991, they did just that. It was a big mistake.

Taking the ball at the 7-yard line, Howard avoided three Buckeye defenders, scooted down the sideline, and streaked into the end zone. Howard then struck a Heisman Trophy pose after the 93-yard punt return, which set a school record. The Heisman Trophy is given to the best football player in the country. It is a bronze statue of a football player sidestepping and straight-arming his way downfield to a mythical touchdown.

"Hello, Heisman!" exclaimed play-by-play announcer Keith Jackson. Hello, indeed. The runback clinched the Heisman Trophy for Howard, one of three won by Michigan players through the years. The others were Tom Harmon (1940) and Charles Woodson (1997).

Charles Woodson starred on defense, offense, and special teams for Michigan from 1995 to 1997.

Michigan opened the 1997 season with blowouts of Colorado and Baylor. Playing on both sides of the ball, Woodson made an impact both offensively and defensively.

By the time the Wolverines reached the final game of the regular season against Ohio State, they were 10–0. The AP Poll ranked Michigan number one.

The Buckeyes were a tough opponent. They had only lost one game all year and were ranked number four. A record crowd of 106,982 at Michigan Stadium watched as Woodson put on an amazing performance. He set up Michigan's first touchdown with a 37-yard pass reception. Then he returned a punt 78 yards for a touchdown and intercepted a pass in the end zone. The Wolverines went on to a 20–14 victory.

Woodson was now being considered for one of football's highest honors—the Heisman Trophy. When he was just a child, his dream was to win that award.

"That dream kind of left" when he became a defensive player, said Woodson. A defensive player had never won the Heisman since it was established in 1935. Tennessee quarterback Peyton Manning was considered the likely Heisman winner in 1997. Instead, Woodson indeed took home the award.

Woodson stepped up to the podium at the Downtown Athletic Club in New York with tears in his eyes and accepted the award. "My body

### "THE VICTORS"

He never scored a touchdown, but Louis Elbel made one of the greatest contributions to Michigan football. He was in the stands on Thanksgiving Day in 1898 when Michigan beat Chicago 12–11. It ended a perfect season and gave the Wolverines their first Western Conference championship. The excited Elbel, a music student, wrote a fight song on the train back to Ann Arbor. In April 1899, the public heard the rousing song for the first time. Thus Michigan's famous fight song, "The Victors," was born.

just went limp, I couldn't really move," Woodson said. "I had to grasp what just happened."

It was Michigan's second Heisman in seven years, following Desmond Howard's win in 1991. Now it was time for the Rose Bowl and a meeting with the Washington State Cougars. A victory would give the Wolverines the national championship.

Woodson did not wait long to make his presence known. He intercepted a pass by Washington State quarterback Ryan Leaf in the end zone. It led to a touchdown that tied the game at 7–7. Late in the game, Michigan was clinging to a 21–16 lead. Washington State was on the move. The Cougars had the ball on Michigan's 26-yard line after a 26-yard gain. The clock was stopped momentarily to move the chains.

Two seconds remained. With no timeouts left, Leaf spiked the ball into the ground to stop the clock. But it was too late. The scoreboard clock at the top of the Rose Bowl stadium showed nothing but zeros.

The Washington State fans wanted to know what happened. They felt cheated. But when Leaf appealed to an official, the referee just shook his head.

Michigan quarterback Brian Griese was voted player of the game after passing for three touchdowns and 251 yards. "It's something kids dream about," Griese said. "I never wanted to be the all-star quarterback. I just wanted to be a part of the team." Griese's father, an all-pro quarterback, had performed on the very same field for Purdue.

The Wolverines and their fans celebrated their first national championship since 1948. Carr never approached another national title, although his run in 13 years in the Big Ten was largely successful. After 1997, his Michigan teams won four conference championships, in 1998, 2000, 2003, and 2004. And the Wolverines never missed a bowl game during his time in Ann Arbor. Teams must win at least six games to be selected for a bowl game.

The Wolverines went into a slump after Rich Rodriguez took over the team in 2008. He was fired after three years. Michigan was

**Michigan quarterback Denard Robinson rushes for a touchdown during a 2011 game against Minnesota.**

a combined 15–22 under Rodriguez, and it never finished better than seventh in the Big Ten.

Brady Hoke replaced Rodriguez as the Michigan coach in 2011. He led the Wolverines to an 11–2 record, featuring a 40–34 win over Ohio State. "This program has been starving," said Michigan quarterback Denard Robinson. "It's time to eat."

Hoke was named Big Ten coach of the year in his very first season. The Wolverines were finding their way back to the top, once again among the elite teams in college football.

# TIMELINE

**1879**

Michigan plays and wins its first intercollegiate football game on May 30 against Racine College at White Stocking Park in Chicago.

**1901**

Fielding Yost begins his long term of service as Michigan football coach with his famous "Point-a-Minute" teams.

**1902**

Michigan appears in the first Rose Bowl on January 1, defeating Stanford by a score of 49–0. The victory gives the Wolverines their first national title.

**1902**

Michigan wins its second national title after an 11–0 season.

**1903**

Michigan shares the national championship with Princeton. Michigan and Penn share the title the next year.

**1940**

Tom Harmon wins Michigan's first Heisman Trophy.

**1947**

Fritz Crisler, who helped create the two-platoon system, leads the "Mad Magicians" to the national championship.

**1948**

Bennie Oosterbaan takes over for Crisler and promptly leads the Wolverines to a second straight championship.

**1950**

Michigan beats Ohio State 9–3 in the infamous "Snow Bowl" in Columbus, Ohio. Blizzard conditions prevail throughout, and teams are forced to punt a combined 45 times.

**1969**

The Wolverines hire Bo Schembechler to take over as head coach. He remains on the job for 21 years, becoming one of the most popular coaches in Michigan history.

**1918**

Michigan and Pittsburgh are recognized as co-national champions.

**1923**

Michigan shares the top spot with Illinois as Yost wins his sixth and final national championship.

**1927**

Michigan Stadium opens on October 1.

**1932**

Coach Harry Kipke leads the Wolverines to the national championship, sharing the title with USC. Michigan stands alone as Kipke wins a second straight title the next year.

**1938**

Herbert O. "Fritz" Crisler is appointed head football coach and assistant director of athletics. He brings the famed winged helmet to Michigan.

**1986**

Schembechler passes Yost as Michigan's all-time leader in wins, earning his 166th victory with the Wolverines in a 26–24 win over Ohio State.

**1991**

Desmond Howard wins the Heisman Trophy.

**1997**

Under Lloyd Carr, the Wolverines win their first national title since 1948. Charles Woodson becomes the third Michigan player to win the Heisman.

**2008**

A 48–42 loss to Purdue assures Michigan of its first losing season in 41 years and ends the program's bowl streak at 33 years.

**2011**

Brady Hoke takes over for Rich Rodriguez and leads the Wolverines to an 11–2 record and a victory in the Sugar Bowl.

# QUICK STATS

## PROGRAM INFO
University of Michigan (1879–98)
University of Michigan Wolverines (1899– )

## NATIONAL CHAMPIONSHIPS
### (*DENOTES SHARED TITLE)
1901, 1902, 1903*, 1904*, 1918*, 1923*, 1932* 1933, 1947, 1948, 1997*

## OTHER ACHIEVEMENTS
BCS bowl appearances (1999– ): 5
Big Ten championships (1917– ): 42
Bowl record: 20–21

## HEISMAN TROPHY WINNERS
Tom Harmon, 1940
Desmond Howard, 1991
Charles Woodson, 1997

## KEY PLAYERS
### (POSITION[S]; SEASONS WITH TEAM)
Anthony Carter (WR; 1979–82)
Bob Chappuis (HB; 1942, 1946–47)
Braylon Edwards (WR; 2001–04)
Tom Harmon (HB; 1938–40)
William Heston (HB; 1901–04)
Desmond Howard (WR; 1989–91)
Ron Johnson (HB; 1966–68)
Ron Kramer (OL; 1954–56)
Bennie Oosterbaan (E-WR; 1925–27)
Charles Woodson (DB; 1995–97)

## KEY COACHES
Lloyd Carr (1995–2007):
122–40–0; 6–7 (bowl games)
Bo Schembechler (1969–89):
194–48–5; 5–12 (bowl games)
Fielding H. Yost (1901–26):
165–29–10; 1–0 (bowl games)

## HOME STADIUM
Michigan Stadium (1927– )

* All statistics through 2011 season

# QUOTES & ANECDOTES

Charles Gayley was a new student at Michigan in 1876. He had traveled in England and Ireland and loved rugby. He was happy to see that US students were playing a game similar to rugby called "foot-ball." But there was one problem: they were playing with too many players. He suggested rugby rules with one exception. Use only 11 players on each side, just the same as Harvard and Yale. With the new rules, the modern era of football was on its way.

Superstardom vs. education? Aaron Ward, a former Michigan hockey player, found out just where Bo Schembechler stood on the subject. Ward had been invited by the Michigan football coach to play in a golf tournament. "We had just won the Stanley Cup and it wasn't, 'Hey, Aaron, congratulations on the Stanley Cup.' He looked at me, plain as day, put his hand out and said, 'When are you going to finish your degree?'" There were no congratulations.

The Wolverines prepared for the Rose Bowl following the 1901 season in Waterman Gymnasium. The team did indoor work in the gymnasium and ran plays outside. Michigan coach Fielding Yost had an idea: build a facility with high ceilings and a dirt floor. The building could be used for practices. It was built 24 years later and called a "field house." Field houses are now standard among major football teams.

# GLOSSARY

**All-American**
A player chosen as one of the best amateurs in the country in a particular activity.

**athletic director**
An administrator who oversees the coaches, players, and teams of an institution.

**conference**
In sports, a group of teams that plays each other each season.

**intercollegiate**
Between different colleges.

**legendary**
Something that is extremely famous, especially in a particular field.

**recruiting**
Trying to entice a player to come to a certain school.

**retired**
Officially ended one's career.

**rival**
An opponent that brings out great emotion in a team, its fans, and its players.

**rivalry**
When opposing teams bring out great emotion in each team, its fans, and its players.

**roster**
The players as a whole on a football team.

# FOR MORE INFORMATION

## FURTHER READING

Chengelis, Angelique. *100 Things Michigan Fans Should Know & Do Before They Die.* Chicago: Triumph Books, 2009.

Falk, Jon. *If These Walls Could Talk: Michigan Football Stories from the Big House.* Chicago: Triumph Books, 2010.

Green, Jerry. *University of Michigan Football Vault: The History of the Wolverines.* Atlanta, GA: Whitman Pub., 2008.

## WEB LINKS

To learn more about the Michigan Wolverines, visit ABDO Publishing Company online at **www.abdopublishing.com**. Web sites about the Wolverines are featured on our Book Links page. These links are routinely monitored and updated to provide the most current information available.

## PLACES TO VISIT

**College Football Hall of Fame**
111 South St. Joseph St.
South Bend, IN 46601
1-800-440-FAME (3263)
**www.collegefootball.org**

This hall of fame and museum highlights the greatest players and moments in the history of college football. Fielding Yost and Tom Harmon are among the former Wolverines enshrined here.

**Michigan Stadium**
1 East Stadium Blvd.
Ann Arbor, MI 48104-3722
313-936-9345
**www.mgoblue.com/facilities/michigan-stadium.html**

This has been Michigan's home field since 1927. In 2011, the stadium, also known as the "Big House," was the largest college football stadium in the United States.

Baylor, 37
Biakabutuka, Tim, 35–36
Big House. *See Michigan Stadium*
Buffalo, 14

California, 20
Carr, Lloyd (coach), 35–36, 40
Chappuis, Bob, 22–23
Crisler, Fritz (coach), 8, 20, 22

Elbel, Louis, 38
Elliot, Charles "Bump," 22, 23, 24–25
Elliot, Pete, 24
Evashevski, Forest "Evy," 19, 20

Ferry Field, 30
Ford, Gerald, 7
Friedman, Benny, 17

Gallon, Jeremy, 8
Griese, Brian, 40

Harmon, Tommy, 7, 19–21, 36
Hayes, Woody, 27–30, 32–33
Heisman Trophy, 21, 32, 36, 38–39
Heston, Willie, 15–16
Hirsch, Elroy "Crazy Legs," 22
Hoke, Brady (coach), 9, 41
Howard, Desmond, 36, 39

Killian, Tim, 32
Kipke, Harry (coach), 17
Koceski, Leo, 24

Little Brown Jug, 28

Michigan Stadium, 5, 7, 11, 16, 30, 38
Moorhead, Don, 32

Ohio State, 21, 23, 24, 27, 28–29, 30–31, 32, 36, 37, 41
Oosterbaan, Bennie, 7, 17, 24

Pond, Irving Kane, 14

Ray, Marcus, 35
Regents Field, 30
Robinson, Denard, 7–8, 10–11, 41
Rodriguez, Rich (coach), 40–41
Rose Bowl, 15–16, 23–24, 32, 35, 39–40
Roundtree, Roy, 9–10

Schembechler, Bo (coach), 27–33, 35
Smith, Vincent, 8
Snow, Neil, 15–16
Stanford, 13, 15–16

Weeks, Harrison "Boss," 15
Weisenburger, Jack, 22, 23
Woodson, Charles, 36–39

Yerges, Howard, 22, 23
Yost, Fielding "Hurry Up" (coach), 11, 13–14, 15, 16–17, 28, 30

## ABOUT THE AUTHOR

Ken Rappoport is a professional sportswriter with more than 50 books to his credit in both the adult and young readers' field. Working for The Associated Press in New York for 30 years, he wrote about every major sport and was the AP's national hockey writer for 14 seasons. Along with the Stanley Cup playoffs and the NHL All-Star Games, he covered the World Series, the Olympic Games, the Final Four, and the NBA Finals, among other assignments. Rappoport has been cited for his work in the young adult field and has written extensively for magazines.